RIGOR FOR GIFTED LEARNERS: MODIFYING CURRICULUM WITH INTELLECTUAL INTEGRITY

Bertie Kingore

Cheryll M. Adams, Series Editor

National Association for Gifted Children

1331 H Street, NW, Suite 1001

Washington, DC 20005

202-785-4268

http://www.nagc.org

TABLE OF CONTENTS

INTRODUCTION

Many educators differentiate less for gifted students than for struggling students. The intensity of today's standards may increase that disparity unless teachers access practical research- and evidence-based strategies to promote differentiation for gifted and potentially gifted students while implementing standards with intellectual integrity. Current standards including the Common Core State Standards (CCSS) and the Next Generation Science Standards (NGSS), fail to define the intervention methods necessary to support and challenge students who function well above grade-level expectations. This book explains the continuous learning needs of high-ability learners and offers research-based, high-yield instructional strategies, curricular modifications, and social-emotional interventions that effectively enhance gifted students' success. Since assessment drives instruction, this book also includes assessments aligned to learning targets and gifted characteristics to document deeper understanding. The content guides educators to differentiate standards and promote a level of intellectual work commensurate with the capabilities of highly capable students. This work is elaborated with anecdotes, examples, practical strategies, applications, resources to augment recommended intervention strategies, and research references that enable readers to realistically extend applications with gifted students in rigorous learning environments.

For linguistic variety and in recognition of the inclusive terminology preferred in many schools, this book uses several different terms interchangeably. *Gifted, high ability, highly capable, advanced, high potential,* and *potentially gifted children* are all used to describe learners of all ages and from all populations who require pace and level acceleration in their instructional services to experience continuous academic learning.

CHAPTER 1: RIGOR FOR GIFTED LEARNERS TODAY

A rigorous learning environment that ensures continuous learning for all students requires educators to develop a clearer understanding of what academic rigor intends and how it can create high expectations and success for advanced and gifted students. To develop the 21st century skills of high-ability students, educators must analyze standards-based shifts in learning and differentiate standards to promote academic growth and appropriate levels of intellectual work.

Educators today are charged with fostering rigorous learning environments to implement high-stakes standards or the Common Core (CCSS) with all students. The majority of these educators also seek practices ensuring that gifted and potentially gifted students' readiness, interests, and different ways of learning are not ignored during this quest for rigor. In 2013, Catherine Gewertz[1] reported that educators are least prepared to teach the CCSS to the subgroups of students who perform either above or below the typical student at a particular grade level.

What Rigor is and is Not for Gifted Learners
When used in an educational context, rigor denotes a greater concern for conceptual thinking rather than memorization as well as quality rather than quantity. In reality, rigor is not one standard in a classroom; rather, it is a variable that increases in response to individual progress. Figure 1.1 presents a comparison to clarify what the concept

of academic rigor intends versus what some misconstrue it
to be.

FIGURE 1.1:
Rigor: What It Is and What it is Not

It is:

1. Relevant and realistic learning experiences with real-world connections.
2. Academic challenges that promote deeper meaning.
3. In-depth thinking about the content.
4. Continuous learning for all students.
5. An expectation for all students to excel at higher levels.
6. A vital component of differentiation.
7. Future-directed: "how can we adapt current instruction so students develop the skills and thinking abilities needed to succeed in future roles?"

It is NOT:

1. Synthetic, graded learning assignments required at specified junctures of learning.
2. Difficult tasks for the sake of them being "rigorous."
3. Continued practice at levels already mastered.
4. Limited to mastery of grade-level standards and core curriculum.
5. Labeling who can and cannot achieve.
6. Something extra to incorporate into the curriculum.
7. President-oriented: "Which current learning standards and core curriculum concepts do students need to master to advance to the next grade level?"

Adapted from: Kingore, B. (2013). *Rigor and Engagement for Growing Minds.* Austin, TX: PA Publishing.

Rigor is relevant when it emerges from authentic rather than synthetic learning experiences and promotes complex connections of core knowledge to real-world applications. It raises high-level but realistic expectations for all students. Through their efforts, students are expected to achieve and potentially excel beyond minimum competency. Rigor and engagement are significant for all students but differ by degree when nurturing gifted and potentially gifted children

Defining Rigor for High-ability Learners

Continuous learning and higher levels of achievement for advanced, gifted, and potentially gifted learners require a rigorous learning environment where these students:

- Engage in high-level learning processes
- Receive support to learn concepts and skills on and beyond grade-level, at a pace commensurate with their capabilities
- Demonstrate their understanding through assessments and high-end products evidencing relevant, sophisticated content

When the instruction of high-ability students is devoid of consistent rigor and engagement, educators risk lower achievement and limited success for these students. Figure 1.2 synthesizes the research confirming potential negative consequences.

Rigor needs to be appropriately infused in curriculum content and instructional practices across grade levels. Educators do not lower expectations for any student; rather, they extend learning opportunities to levels that ensure continuous learning for all students, including high-ability learners.

FIGURE 1.2:
WHAT CAN HAPPEN IF WE FAIL TO NURTURE ADVANCED POTENTIAL?

Without Appropriate Rigor and Engagement, High-Ability Students May Exhibit One or Combinations of the Following Outcomes:

1. Underdeveloped academic habits of mind; less tolerance for the struggle or persistence that promotes advanced learning.
2. Lower achievement gains; limited progress relative to potential.
3. Deterioration of potential skills and decreased enthusiasm for learning.
4. Patterns of underachievement and/or behavior issues.
5. Boredom.
6. Hidden abilities.
7. Decreased personal satisfaction and self-esteem.
8. A fixed mindset.
9. Less productive and engaged lives.

Synthesized from Castellano & Diaz, 2002; Colangelo, Assouline, & Gross, 2004; Dweck, 2006; Ford & Harris, 1999; Slocumb & Payne, 2011; Sousa, 2009; Tomlinson, 2003; Willis, 2010

Kingore, B. (2013). *Rigor and Engagement for Growing Minds*. Austin, TX: PA Publishing.

Standards-based Shifts in Learning

The focus of today's standards transforms the dominant concern of education from solely mastering content to understanding how instruction influences students' deeper understanding, continuous learning, and life after high school. These standards require intensified instructional rigor that shifts toward teaching greater depth of fewer but higher-level concepts in all content areas. In general, the standards define what all students are expected to understand and be able to do, not how teachers should teach.

Currently, the CCSS, NGSS, and other standards fail to define the intervention methods that ensure continuous learning and support systems for students who function well above grade-level expectations or meet standards prior to completing any grade level. Educators need to explore and implement ways to differentiate standards to promote the academic growth of high-ability students and foster their appropriate level of intellectual work.

Technology is a critical 21st century skill, essential to enable students to develop many of the requirements of today's sophisticated standards. The CCSS and NGSS recommend the application of technological skills to incorporate research and digital media skills across curricula and grade levels. This priority is quite relevant for all students but should be differentiated for advanced students in the following ways:

1. Focus on questions that gifted students cannot simply look up on the Internet. Pose complex questions as well as expect advanced students to construct essential questions that require sophisticated resources, multiple step processes, and abstract thinking.

2. Provide advanced support through school technicians and mentors to ensure that gifted students' use of

technology fosters their ability to produce higher-level responses and access higher-learning opportunities, including online college courses.

3. Incorporate technology to strengthen flexible group interactions across classrooms or with virtual teams of intellectual peers to forward gifted students pursuit of advanced information, unique connections in problem solving, higher-level academic conversations, and their development of professional-level projects.

4. Anticipate that the ubiquitous multiple-choice scantrons will be replaced by standardized assessments administered with laptops, computers, or tablets. In all content areas, assessment tasks will require students to analyze and evaluate information, think critically through multiple perspectives, and compose complex, evidence-based written responses using technology.

Interdisciplinary Connections to Standards
Standards establish targets for all disciplines and grade levels that are both specific yet related. Responding to the characteristic transdisciplinary interests of gifted children, it is effective to focus on the interdisciplinary connections that enable educators to address standards in multiple learning situations.

- Current standards emphasize conceptual understanding, evidence-based reasoning, and a culture of explanation rather than a culture of right answers. Explanation necessitates an instructional shift from students merely answering the problem to explaining their thinking and approach used to problem solve. In math and science, for example, this focus enables gifted students to move beyond procedural knowledge toward applying concepts to novel situations that produce original proofs and scientific reports expanding their conceptual underpinnings.

- The CCSS focus on carefully analyzed, evidence-based writing-to-inform across the curriculum challenges high-ability students to marshal evidence from their reading to construct written analytical arguments integrating current real-world themes and issues into traditional learning assignments.
- The CCSS place a high priority on the use of nonfiction and content area literacy to prepare students for real-world data in the workplace. This emphasis aligns with the voracious appetite for nonfiction displayed at an early age by high-ability children, particularly when relevant to their areas of personal interest.
- Respond to the demand for higher text complexity by ensuring that gifted students gain access to a wider range of multiple-level resources providing both complex readability levels and concept density. Concept density stimulates more complex thinking to promote deeper understanding.
- Maximize applications of academic vocabulary to build a sophisticated understanding of the specific terminology in different fields as well as spur students' academic conversations and their ability to express more complex thinking as they construct deeper understanding. Academic vocabulary is also recognized as a direct influence on students' success on high-stakes assessments. Marilee Sprenger identified 55 words critical for students to know to be successful on standardized tests and CCSS assessments.[2]

CHAPTER 2: A COLLABORATIVE LEARNING ENVIRONMENT

A rigorous learning environment requires a climate for learning and relationship building that is characterized by collaboration among all participants. The quality of the personal relationships among adults and peers in a classroom propels students' behavior and advances or impedes their learning. Hence, a collaborative learning environment should focus on instructional priorities that foster productivity and nurture students who care about others while thinking for themselves.

Instructional Priorities
Rigor requires action and changes in instruction. In a rigorous learning environment, educators demonstrate instructional priorities that facilitate higher achievement. The following five instructional priorities enable educators to implement appropriately rigorous practices to benefit all students while promoting high-level, continuous learning for advanced and gifted students.

R-Recognize realistic & relevant high-level expectations
I-Integrate complexity/depth in content, process, & product
G-Generate cognitive skills
O-Orchestrate support systems & scaffold success
R-Refine assessments to guide instruction to benefit learners

Recognize Realistic and Relevant High-level Expectations
In rigorous learning environments, teachers must communicate realistic but high-level expectations that

challenge students to demonstrate effort to advance their own learning. For example, to help students to understand that their effort would result in greater success, one teacher said that she guaranteed that they would learn and advance in her class if they demonstrated daily that they would think, try, and participate in the class learning experiences. This technique set a tone of shared responsibility and realistic expectations for learning. If a student was not making progress despite thinking, trying, and participating, it removed the burden from the student and became a clear indication the teacher needed to approach this learning situation another way. On the other hand, if a potentially gifted student was performing at grade level rather than working toward higher levels, that student and the teacher would conference to initiate discussions of change.

Relevance is crucial to rigor, deeper understanding, and student ownership. Content that is relevant makes more sense to students, enabling them to connect the unknown to what is known and construct deeper meaning. Learning experiences that are relevant stimulate students to assume more ownership in learning because they understand the ways in which this content or skill applies to their lives. Less relevant applications primarily focus on memorizing and reporting facts.

Be vigilant when reviewing the profusion of curricula materials being offered in the name of rigor and the CCSS. Many materials make the learning tasks more difficult but fail to infuse significant relevance. Challenge without relevance produces skeptical and less motivated gifted students.

Relevance is interdisciplinary and connects content to real-world contexts and students' interests through experiences such as the following:

- ☑ Authentic learning applications producing something useful
- ☑ Simulations integrating the social, emotional, and academic aspects of real-world events
- ☑ Teaching others in the classroom or in virtual learning environments
- ☑ Incorporating current or future issues
- ☑ Problem-based and project-based learning
- ☑ Connecting concepts to local, national, or global events
- ☑ Interest-driven inquiry
- ☑ Service learning that meaningfully benefits others

Search your current curriculum and select a few high quality learning experiences that effectively help students learn targeted concepts and skills. Then, challenge yourself to revise each to include more relevant, motivating applications. Some educators use this revision experience to increase interdisciplinary connections to targeted skills, as in Figure 2.1.

With today's digital landscape, students are connected to the world through technology and operate in a multimedia, online, random-access, audio-visual world. According to leaders in technology including Lee Crockett and Marc Prensky, digital access to information implies that it is less relevant or realistic to expect today's students to know every accumulated detail.[3] It is more relevant that they understand the big ideas of the content, the overreaching concepts,

FIGURE 2.1:
TRADITIONAL VS. MORE RELEVANT APPLICATION OF
SKILLS AND CONCEPTS

TRADITIONAL ASSIGNMENT

Language Arts: Read nonfiction resources to learn about fruits and vegetables; Create an alphabet book that includes information about a fruit or vegetable for every letter.

Math: Write and illustrate original math problems using area and perimeter.
Science: Complete a three-way Venn diagram comparing three biomes.

Social Sciences: Create a class collage of jobs that are significant to a community's welfare.

MORE RELEVANT APPLICATION

Language Arts: After reading resources about vegetable gardens, write an evidence-based sequenced plan for how to make a roof-top or in-ground garden at school.

Math: Design a school garden with an irrigation system that maximizes growing capacity in the smallest space. Prepare a budget for purchasing materials and supplies.

Science: Research flora indigenous to the area of the biome in which you live. Plant a school garden with useful herbs and other vegetables matched to ground conditions and area weather.
Social Sciences: Research and organize where and how school-grown vegetables can be donated or most productively used for the betterment of the community.

Adapted from: Kingore, B. (2013). *Rigor and Engagement for Growing Minds.* Austin, TX: PA Publishing.

and how to access, comprehend, and scrutinize needed data.

> **Application: Integrate Relevant Interests**
> Ask students to write a list of ten to twenty
> personal interests to keep in a work folder. When
> appropriate, end a segment of learning by asking
> students, "Which one of your interests can you
> connect to this information? Explain."

Integrate Complexity and Depth in Content, Process, and Product

Complexity and depth entail more than higher levels of thinking. Complexity denotes a focus on concepts leading to intricate interconnections of ideas, problems, and issues across disciplines. Depth denotes extensive and detailed study within the layers of a discipline from concrete to abstract and from concepts to generalizations. Combined, they represent the comprehensive and thorough understanding expected in a rigorous learning environment,

Consider the following questions. The first is a good question inviting high-level thinking. The second set elicits complexity and depth requiring high-level thinking within the larger framework of conceptual structures and big ideas.

> ***High-level thinking question:*** "What combination of historical factors influenced the establishment of the Underground Railroad?"
>
> ***High-level concept questions:*** "Which concept had the greatest impact on the Underground Railroad: power, survival, or beliefs? Explain." "In what ways was the function of the Underground Railroad like the function of online social networks today? Supply evidence.

Advanced students operate at higher levels of complexity and depth when they apply and adapt concept-based learning. Increased complexity and depth in content, process, and product are likely when teachers facilitate students' applications of concepts, principles, and generalizations through investigations of fuzzy, real-world problems having interdisciplinary and multifaceted solutions.

To maximize opportunities for complexity and depth, students must be responsible for designing the process, content, and products of relevant problem-solving experiences rather than merely completing a learning task designed by the teacher. For example, students identify a school-related problem, such as a dangerous traffic crossing. They devise procedures using digital cameras to record data, edit, organize the data graphically, identify the person with the power to initiate change, and then write and present a substantiated, factual report to that person.

- Facilitate complexity and depth for gifted students by providing fiction and nonfiction resources that exceed grade-level.

- Scaffold deeper comprehension of expository text by adding a section across the bottom of concept maps, graphs, and Venn diagrams. Ask gifted students to complete the graphic with a summary, conclusion, or generalization. This recomposing from a graphic to linguistic format requires students to process the content in a different way and elicits deeper meaning.
- Advanced students benefit from discussions regarding how an intellectual person needs to cautiously consider ways the digital culture both improves and hinders our lives. Support students as they learn to be vigilant consumers accessing and documenting authenticity of websites that enable advanced explorations with greater complexity, breadth, and depth relating to their interests and topics of study.
- Increase complexity and depth by documenting when advanced students have mastered content and allowing them to proceed with higher-level replacement learning tasks instead of engaging in redundant practice. In-depth study is a productive differentiation strategy and an effective replacement task that empowers an advanced student to extend personal learning at a level and pace uniquely suited to that person as a scholar. As students increase independence to develop and investigate authentic problems, they refine more sophisticated self-management, research skills, and productive habits of mind. As they interpret and adapt the ideas they discover, they develop enduring skills and higher-level understanding of new concepts and ideas derived from the inquiry.

- Integrating higher-level vocabulary increases content complexity and depth. Research supports academic vocabulary as one of the strongest indicators of how well students learn subject-area content. For example, Gifford and Gore found that immersing middle school students in specific math vocabulary resulted in higher levels of achievement and an increased pace of learning.[4] Higher cognitive processing requires high-level academic vocabulary specific to content fields.

Reflective Moment

James Stronge asserts that students learn more when taught by teachers with greater verbal ability who use authentic contextual applications of language than when taught by teachers with lower verbal ability.[5] In what ways do you agree or disagree with this statement?

Generate Cognitive Skills

Although a lengthy subset of skills can be included in cognitive skills, Ned Noddings suggests that most teachers relate cognitive skills to the mental activity that uses facts to seek meaning and uses reasoning to question and form judgments.[6] When discussing cognitive skills, standards often distinguish among critical thinking, creative thinking, literacy skills, and reflective thinking. However, cognitive skills are interdependent and rarely function alone. Particularly with gifted students, I encourage cognitive flexibility and adaptability to emphasize the creative mental activity that explores new relationships while using cognitive skills to question the known, inject new possibilities, and tackle problems in a diverse fashion.

Advanced students activate high-level cognitive skills when they are challenged to apply knowledge to novel or unique situations, particularly when the task involves a complex, unpredictable problem. They also engage cognitive skills as they infer to derive a logical conclusion on the basis of partial evidence and reasoning. Through inference, highly capable learners integrate high-level thinking skills such as synthesis, interpretation, logic, and abstract thinking into educated projections accompanied with supporting evidence. This mental activity simultaneously increases their understanding of the whole as they infer additional meaning.

Teachers should promote cognitive applications that evidence the dispositions of curiosity and open-mindedness across disciplines for all age levels and throughout learning experiences. To consistently generate cognitive skills during instruction, educators need to emphasize cognitive strategies, such as high-level thinking, questioning, analogous and comparative thinking, and summarization.

High-level Thinking: Key Points

1. Filter our terminology. Inasmuch as the term *low* connotes a more negative skill, refer to Bloom's taxonomy as eliciting beginning-to-high levels of thinking rather than low-to-high levels.

2. Frequently engage all students in the process of high-level thinking.

3. Tier the complexity and depth of *analyze, evaluate,* and *create* for advanced students.

Similar to the social studies examples in Figure 2.2, analytical thinking can apply to content that is more concrete (Tier 1) or more complex and abstract (Tier 2). Ensure opportunities for highly capable students to engage in thinking processes requiring greater complexity, depth, and abstract thinking in multi-dimensional, unpredictable situations.

Figure 2.2:
Tiered High-Level Thinking in Social Studies

Analysis Tier 1	Analysis Tier 2
What aspects of the topography enabled this population to settle in this location?	Discuss this historical event from the perspectives of three different participants.
Explain three similarities and differences related to the history of these two cultures.	Using past and present conditions, predict and compare future cultural trends for these two cultures.

Adapted from: Kingore, B. (2013). *Rigor and Engagement for Growing Minds*. Austin, TX: PA Publishing.

Questioning

A generation ago, classroom questioning involved the teacher asking students questions to determine who knew or who did not know predetermined answers. Today, the greater purpose of questioning is to help students refine their thinking and conceptual development as we assess their perceptions, misconceptions, and depth of information. Thus, questioning provides formative assessment information that enables us to productively adjust the pace and level of instruction.

- Use open-ended questions, such as those below, that guide students to bring their thinking to a conscious level and discuss a current strategy or action that they can then invoke at a different time for refining or application.
  "How did you figure that out?"
  "What evidence do you have to support that?"
  "What question is essential to this topic?"
  "If this is the correct answer, what is the mathematical (or scientific) question?"
- Focus on text-dependent, concept-based questions that cannot be answered with prior knowledge or with one quick reference to the Internet.
- Avoid asking, "Does anyone have a question?" Instead, prime the brain by first inviting students to discuss possible questions for a minute with a shoulder partner. Then, ask the group, *"What possible questions emerged from your thinking?"*

Application: The Language of High-level Thinking
Challenge gifted students to incorporate the language of high-level thinking and logical reasoning in their academic conversations. Purposefully using terminology such as *analyze, use logic to, identify a new relationship, interpret,* and *prioritize* in contextual conversations reinforces vocabulary and the process of their reasoning.

Analogies and Comparative Thinking

While no instructional strategy is equally effective in all situations and with all populations, research updated by Ceri Dean and others indicates that identifying similarities and differences is one of the most significant strategies for increasing students' achievement.[7] Since analogies are the most complex format for comparative thinking, they merit particular attention for application by high-ability students.

1. Oral analogies invite students to verbally compare a concrete item with current content and are usually expressed as a simile or metaphor. For example, display an object the children clearly recognize and promote depth by requesting how many different connections they can make to the present topic of study such as, *"How many ways is this water bottle like our bodies?"*

2. Direct analogies are thought-provoking tools to tease out inferences. They facilitate long-term memory by requiring students to create meaningful connections instead of focus on memorizing facts. *"John Steinbeck's _____ is a time capsule of the Great Depression just as Harriet Beecher Stowe's _____ is _____. "*

3. Personal analogies are a variation of direct analogies in which students connect themselves to a content-related object or topic. This form increases relevancy by promoting a social, emotional response to content, as with the open-ended prompt that follows. The second example is an analogy from a secondary student sharing his perspective of being gifted. *"I am like the antagonist when _____."* *"Gifted kids are a square light bulb. They are bright, unique, but need a regular bulb base as eventually they have to fit into the real world."*

Summarization

Summarization is a cognitive process that requires students to synthesize information for long-term memory. Judy Willis, a neurologist, explains that when students condense textual main ideas and connections the mental activity that occurs actually consolidates constructed information into existing memory circuits.[8] Research substantiates that summarizing is pertinent to most lessons and remains one of the most significant strategies for increasing students' achievement.[9] Since summarization has such a powerful effect on memory and since gifted students prefer minimum repetition in learning situations, they greatly benefit when they acquire extensive skill in summarization.

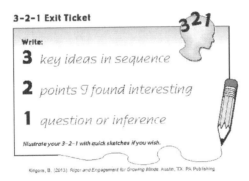

3-2-1 Exit Ticket

Write:

3 key ideas in sequence

2 points I found interesting

1 question or inference

Illustrate your 3-2-1 with quick sketches if you wish.

Kingore, B. (2013). Rigor and Engagement for Growing Minds. Austin, TX: PA Publishing

- Maintain relevancy and students' interest in summarization by implementing it with widely varied instructional applications for novelty. For example, occasionally use a 3-2-1 Exit Ticket as a scaffold to promote summarization.
- Brain research suggests that factual lectures should be broken into shorter segments to maximize student attention.[10] After eight to fifteen minutes, facilitate a summarization task before returning to

the lecture format. While this process may seem to require more class time, teachers save repetitive instruction later because students retain more of the information.

> **Application: Inference**
>
> Challenge gifted students to discuss the significant role of inference in ethics, interdisciplinary topics, and global issues. Consider the pluses and minuses, and interesting aspects of the connections people infer related to their perspective, bias, prejudice, and motive.

Orchestrate Support Systems and Scaffold Success

Gifted children think differently; they also feel differently. Their emotional intensity results in heightened awareness and qualitatively different ways of perceiving the world. They can experience alienation at school when they perceive that they are markedly different from age peers. For their emotional, social, and academic well-being, it is imperative that educators, families, and peers understand these differences as normal for advanced learners. This human support system should help gifted students interact with and learn from intellectual peers as well as age peers so they feel accepted, understood, respected, and supported by others.

Grouping is not, nor should it be, a stagnant destination inasmuch as students benefit from participating in diverse group placements during learning opportunities. To experience challenge, however, highly capable students

FIGURE 2.3:
INTELLECTUAL PEERS

Flexible Groups of Intellectual Peers Enable Advanced Students to:

- Pursue the intellectual risk taking needed to succeed in advanced study.
- Search out higher-level resources and experience advanced academic work that is relevant, stimulating, and intellectually challenging rather than engage in redundant work.
- Academically advance at a pace commensurate to their readiness and rate of learning.
- Post complex questions as well as respond to hard questions from peers that require securing evidence from advanced resources, critical thinking, insight, and thoughtful reflection.
- Respectfully interact with peers who are also interested in more sophisticated word choices and choose to respond with greater depth while engaging in demanding learning processes.
- Experience the social and emotional peer support they deserve while developing self-awareness and resiliency.

Adapted from: Kingore, B. (2013). *Rigor and Engagement for Growing Minds*. Austin, TX: PA Publishing.

must confront a problem they have not yet encountered and interact with intellectual peers as well as age peers. To minimize any counterproductive attention to intellectual peers, schedule these groups to work together while the rest of the class is also in small groups using different levels of content materials or pursuing different concepts.

Refine Assessments to Guide Instruction and Benefit Learners

Academic rigor is driven by high expectations, but it requires educators to scaffold support and provide feedback to enable students to fulfill those expectations. While all students need instructional support, the degree and kind of support varies in response to individual students and the academic opportunities they have experienced. Figure 2.4 suggests instructional support strategies needed by all students compared to additional strategies pivotal to supporting advanced and gifted students

The interdependent relationship among assessment, instruction, and achievement is evident. In effective rigorous learning environments, educators implement multifaceted, continual assessment to guide instructional decisions, document deeper understanding, and facilitate students' success through actionable data aligned to learning targets and gifted characteristics. This focus ensures that gifted students experience continuous learning and maintain records of progress reflecting personal changes as learners. Jay McTighe and Ken O'Connor reminds us that assessment should produce data to evidence initial understanding, calculate progress, and provide beneficial feedback for students' reflection and self-assessment.[11]

- A simple way to promote rigor with high-ability students is by implementing more complex levels of

Figure 2.4:
Instructional Support Strategies

ALL Students Benefit from these Strategies:

- Form interest groups so students mutually engage each other in personally relevant content.
- Use flexible groups for discussions, problem solving and hands-on applications to maintain a dynamic learning environment.
- Provide online or classroom videos of lecture information so students can learn at their best pace.
- Develop academic vocabulary to enhance comprehension and cognitive processing.
- Foster critical thinking and explanation to promote deeper understand.

In Addition, these Strategies are Crucial to Support Highly Capable Students:

- When feasible, accelerate instructional pace and level to avoid intellectual stagnation.
- Allow student choice and self-nomination for challenging replacement tasks that develop personal areas of giftedness and interests.
- Solicit mentors either on-site or through technology.
- Ensure access to gifted intellectual peers in class or across classrooms.
- Provide websites and resources that promote complexity, depth, and more abstract thinking while enabling access to content that exceeds grade-level.

Adapted from: Kingore, B. (2013). *Rigor and Engagement for Growing Minds*. Austin, TX: PA Publishing.

authentic assessments that measure responses exceeding grade-level expectations.

- Use assessments that document the acquisition of targeted standards while challenging advanced students to question, adapt, and extend as much as master core curricula content. For example, assess mathematical understanding by requiring a student to justify why a sophisticated mathematical statement or problem solution is valid.
- To yield a far more accurate assessment of the range, depth, and quality of students' accomplishments and changes as learners, assess work that extends over time and substantiates individual intellectual work, such as the stages of a research project or experiment. Additional examples of work over time include narrative assessment logs of intellectual accomplishments with personal and utilitarian value, portfolios of sophisticated product examples, and evidenced-based applications of theories to solve real-life problems.

Since rigor is concerned with quality, the volume of assignments is less significant than the merit of the tasks. If a certain number of grades are required by outside decision makers, respond by breaking a long-term assignment into smaller units for evaluations. For example, evaluate the student's plan and procedure for a learning project to determine a grade and to provide formative feedback recommending potential changes before the next phase of the task continues.

Rubrics have been widely used and perfected by teachers over the last 30 years. Building on prior successful experiences with rubrics, expand the value and effective implementation of rubrics as both assessment tools (contributing information for instructional decisions) and evaluation instruments (grading learning products or processes).

> **Instead of:** ▪Correct information ▪Accurate applications of skills ▪Followed directions ▪Completed on time ▪Neat
>
> **Emphasize:** ▶In-depth information ▶Conceptual ideas ▶Complex ideas ▶Academic vocabulary ▶Extends learning for self

- Understand that teachers' feedback to students has a direct and powerful effect on student' interpretations of what is valued in learning environments. Analyze your collection of rubrics to determine if you clearly communicate to students what is expected and valued in a rigorous learning environment. Some teachers realize that, unintentionally, their rubrics emphasize accuracy and appearance more than complexity, conceptual thinking, and depth of content.
- At the bottom of rubrics, add space for action statements to provide opportunities for student reflection and empowerment to reach higher expectations. Students conclude their self-assessment on a rubric by goal setting and planning action for continued learning. Specifically, ask gifted students to explain how they exceeded expectations or incorporated a personal connection to the assigned task.

Engaging Students

Engaged students are actively on task in their thinking and participating in the process of learning–the opposite, for example, of trying to learn the game of football strictly from lecture and a playbook. Engagement is crucial. David Sousa contends that how students engage in the work is more significant to long-term memory and learning dispositions than the number of assignments students complete.[12]

Applications from brain research by experts including David Sousa, Judy Willis, Carol Tomlinson, and John Medina provide insights into many aspects of engagement or the lack of it in classrooms.[13] To ensure a productive level of engagement, guide instructional decisions with research implications, such as the following:

- ☑ Novelty helps to shift brains to full attention.
- ☑ A healthy social and emotional learning environment is paramount to students' resilience and higher cognitive engagement.
- ☑ Students expedite deeper understanding when they actively adapt or incorporate information as they construct new relationships in different forms, such as from linguistic to graphic.
- ☑ Physical activity heightens concentration and boosts brainpower with the flow of oxygen-rich blood to the brain.
- ☑ Sustain mental engagement by organizing concentrated lecture into multiple segments of less than fifteen minutes, interspersed with student interaction and application between segments.

Ponder this question when planning instruction, "How can I engage advanced students in constructing deeper meaning and applying targeted knowledge and skills beyond grade-level understanding?" The answer is not to determine some tangentially related activity for them to do for a few minutes; the answer is to connect content and engagement for more rigorous results. For example, student reflection or responses to questions is more engaging, richer, and more meaningful if students first think together in pairs to prime their brains. Additionally, when we ask students to figure out a problem or example, invite engagement and simultaneously honor introspective learners by announcing, "You may work by yourself or with one or two others." For example, rather than merely give students a set of math problems to complete, engage them in flexible groups to formulate their own examples of real-life problems that apply targeted skill and concept sets so math becomes useful and used.

Ultimately, engagement is a response to the structured freedom in a collaborative learning environment where gifted and potentially gifted students feel ownership in learning decisions. Combinations of several factors align with gifted characteristics to heighten student engagement in learning situations.

> **Reflective Moment:** Richard Jones states that it is primarily the teacher's responsibility to engage the students, as opposed to the teacher expecting students to come to class naturally and automatically ready to engage.[14] In what ways do you agree or disagree with this statement?

Factors of Student Engagement
Personal Relationships. With high-ability students, social and emotional difficulties diminish and intellectual risk

taking accelerates when students feel respected by teachers and peers.

Peer Interaction. In a rigorous learning environment, learning experiences should be spelled exPEERiences to denote the importance and motivation of peer interactions in real-life problem solving.

Technology. Technology is inherently engaging to today's digital learners. Through technology, high-ability learners experience more cognitively demanding work as they collaborate on virtual teams, have access to mentors beyond the classroom, and participate in advanced online classes.

Relevancy, Interests, and Choice. Offer choices in learning experiences and products so students can select options more relevant to them and their best ways to demonstrate learning. Choice increases student motivation to exert the effort required to excel. Gifted students flourish through opportunities to apply targeted concepts and skills in their self-selected, self-directed, interest-driven inquiry and projects.

Inquisitiveness. Curiosity fosters engagement. Inquisitive interactions elicit strong reactions among students or between a student and content materials.

Activity and Visual Applications. During instruction, brain research encourages teachers to engage today's digital learners with physical movement, hands-on learning tasks, project-based learning, and visual applications such as graphic organizers, photographs, art, videos, and technology.

Variety, Novelty, or Humor. These elements wake-up the brain. They are a call to attention and memory as students are more inclined to remember the unexpected or a funny example rather than a list of facts.

Engaged, Knowledgeable Teachers. Engaged teachers more effectively engage students. When teachers clearly love their profession, obviously care about who they teach, and enthuse a fascination with what they teach, they connect with their students.

Managing a Collaborative Environment

Rather than imply control, the term classroom management should signify a system to stimulate learning. It develops from the collaborative relationships mutually agreed upon by teachers and students, which Maurice Elias contends is the most significant factor in effective classroom management.[15] A collaborative learning environment is characterized by quality instruction that integrates social and emotional learning into the curriculum. Students are empowered with strategies that help them develop the resiliency to respond to future challenging situations and authentically extend learning.

A collaborative plan works effectively when clearly articulated and consistently practiced. With students, establish predictable routines that vest power with everyone in the classroom to ensure that all members work productively, efficiently, and are better able to focus on constructing deeper understanding of content when working independently or in flexible groups without direct teaching. Gifted students who clearly understand and comfortably operate within agreed management guidelines can better promote their own learning and work toward developing autonomy.

- Problem solve with students to develop ways for them to gain assistance without feeling stymied or calling undue attention to themselves.

- Build personal connections with students each day by positioning yourself at the door and using students' first names as they enter and exit.
- Model a volume level and tone that you want students to use. Use your voice as a powerful management tool that can soothe a tempest or stimulate enthusiasm for a segment of learning.
- Collaboratively create a classroom social contract to define the rights and responsibilities of each participant in the classroom. Discuss how to interact positively and disagree diplomatically as part of an effective learning community. Some gifted learners benefit from learning to filter how they phrase complex ideas and responses to avoid alienating listeners operating at different levels of readiness.
- Instill respect. Respect for others and respect for self is a mandate in effective learning environments. Constantly model and promote responsive and respectful interactions among all class members regardless of perceived ability, culture, income, or unique interests.
- Believe students will learn. If we allow ourselves to become sarcastic or skeptical of students, what can we realistically expect from them?
- Model active listening. Face students, maintain eye contact, and quietly attend to them as they offer what they perceive as an important point. Call on students to paraphrase, summarize, review, or respond to positive ideas from peers during a discussion. Provide a reason for peers to listen to each other through advanced cues, such as, *"As _____ shares, listen to be able to build upon one key point."*

- Ask students to help configure furniture to create more inviting collaboration areas and foster students' ownership of the learning environment.
- Initiate a variety of communication avenues for you and students to contact one another outside of the classroom.
- Use closure as a tool to build a community of learners. When students work in flexible groups or simultaneously engage in a variety of different learning tasks, close with a whole-group segment that brings everyone together for debriefing, summarizing, and sharing. Students benefit by recognizing that we do not all learn in the same way at the same time all of the time.
- Collaborate with education colleagues to share management concerns and explore possible solutions relevant to veteran as well as less experienced teachers.

> ***Reflective Moment*** Consider what your school and classroom environment suggest about your educational priorities.

CHAPTER 3: DIFFERENTIATION FOR ADVANCED AND GIFTED STUDENTS

Psychology is at the foundation of human behavior including learning and development in the classroom. An understanding of the psychological principles and their applications allow teachers to base their practices in science. The arts are for everyone and extend throughout the instructional day, not just in special rooms or for special students. They are an integral part of the human experience that can be harnessed not only to enrich students but also to engage students in the day-to-day content and skills we wish students to learn. At the same time, teachers have a responsibility to facilitate the growth of potential artistic contributors. It is not easy to predict who these students will be, so when a little bud presents itself, we need to nurture it. From a psychological perspective this is accomplished by structuring experiences to provide for exploration, stressing the importance of practice and mastery of basic skills, and then giving the older student the courage to try. Respect the arts and the children who engage in them by embracing their potential in your classroom.

Ensure less intensive preparation for differentiation by initiating open-ended learning tasks. When advanced students' respond to open-ended tasks with engagement and diverse, higher cognitive responses, teachers may be receptive to building toward more strategic differentiation with tiered instruction and curriculum compacting. The following suggestions are characterized by less intensive

FIGURE 3.1:

LEARNING STRATEGIES VARIED FOR ENGAGEMENT AND RIGOR

Cooperative Learning	• Jigsaw using advanced-level materials. • Elaborate ideas with symbols reflecting abstract thinking. • Have students evaluate to determine a group achievement that could not be achieved individually.
Think-Pair-Share	• Pair high-ability students for intellectual support with increased content complexity and depth. • Determine and incorporate key academic vocabulary. • Have pairs conclude by determining their two best ideas. • End with each person summarizing the ideas of the other.
Pair-Share-Square	• Reach a consensus of the three best ideas that emerged. • Rank the key points in order of their significance.
Role-Play	• Create a conversation that occurs between two concepts. • Role play conflicts of interests or ethics. • Have students end the experience by writing a brief conclusion based on multiple perspectives.

Adapted from: Kingore, B. (2013). *Rigor and Engagement for Growing Minds*. Austin, TX: PA Publishing.

teacher preparation to empower us (and our sometimes-reluctant and often-overwhelmed colleagues) to successfully differentiate instruction and appropriately increase challenge for highly capable students.

- Simultaneously, incorporate open-ended learning tasks at different levels of complexity by providing two graphic organizers with one eliciting simple, concrete responses and the other eliciting more complex, elaborated interpretations. This selection permits classmates to work at different levels on a similar task and promotes product and content differentiation when you provide different levels of resources.

- To differentiate product, process, and content, collaborate with students to produce and post a list of generalizable, authentic learning applications that students can self-select as products and replacement tasks. Ensure that the tasks include simple to more complex applications. Once established, teachers have a motivating tool for differentiating instruction by responding to individual differences and interests without excessive preparation of projects and inquiry assignments.

- Increase student applications of self-assessment to enable highly-capable students to concretely view their progress and experience a greater incentive to improve academic growth as they aspire to personal best. Researchers including Stiggins and Chappuis support that self-assessment escalates achievement as it necessitates students' increased involvement in their own learning.[16] When advantageous, group intellectual peers to promote more complex, in-depth problem solving among them.

- When using individually selected inquiry or replacement tasks, list targeted skills or concepts and require gifted students to explain when and how they applied each to their interest-driven work.
- As teachers comfortably apply a differentiation strategy, encourage them to share their success with others and build on that success by progressing to another application.
- Encourage colleagues to participate in professional development opportunities that focus on effective ways to manage acceleration and increasingly incorporate elements of complexity and depth into existing lessons.
- Collaborate to change attitudes! Colleagues agree that all students need to learn. Expand that concept to promote the reality that all students have the right to continuous learning at their highest levels of readiness. We have worked for several years to become skilled at supporting struggling learners and that support is needed and appropriate. Now, it is time to also increase our skills in supporting high-ability learners.

Promoting Intellectual Work

To summarize — Rigor is not characterized by more work but by more meaningful work that is intellectually challenging and thought provoking, relative to the developmental age of the child. Students flourish through interactions with intellectual peers as well as age peers to experience a real-world balance between academic challenge and the social and emotional support that promotes resilience and joy in learning. Academic rigor and socialization skills are mutually beneficial.

The Center for Authentic Intellectual Work (AIW) frames intellectual work with three criteria: construction of knowledge, disciplined inquiry, and value beyond school. AIW explains that authentic intellectual work requires original application of knowledge and skills rather than routine applications of facts and procedures.[17]

Students' propensity to engage in intellectual work is an intended outcome of academic rigor. In a rigorous learning environment, educators must promote intellectual work and students must aspire to engage in learning in a manner that displays distinctive attributes of intellectual work similar to those listed in Figure 3.2. These attributes enable students to grow as resilient learners who adapt current knowledge to prepare for future academic and workplace cultures.

Intellectual work leads children of all ages to a deep immersion in a subject over time, using sophisticated resources with the guidance of expert practitioners or mentors. Mature students function more like academicians and clinicians who remain committed to their work as they encounter complex, unpredictable problems and are subject to peer and public scrutiny. The demands of their academic process cause them to continuously expand their levels of skills as they construct deeper, more complex understanding, develop self-awareness and resiliency, and increasingly assume ownership of their ideas and actions. There several ways to provide authentic intellectual work suitable for gifted students in the general school setting.

FIGURE 3.2:
ATTRIBUTES OF INTELLECTUAL WORK

Students' Intellectual Work in a Rigorous Learning Environment:

- Is meaningful, high quality, intellectually challenging work accompanied by appropriate support.
- Has an authentic purpose relevant to the learner that motivates a reason to exert effort and strive for a remarkable accomplishment.
- Requires substantive peer and adult interactions with elaborated communication through complex, multifaceted forms.
- Incorporates prodigious experiences with strategic reading of nonfiction texts and generation of evidence-based writing to assess and support their construction of deeper meaning.
- Leads students to become producers, constructing new knowledge and conceptual, in-depth understanding with increasing sophistication in process and product.
- Develops a structure of knowing rather than only memorizing known details.
- Demonstrates intellectual openness, creativity, and commitment that lead to a state of flow with a contagious excitement for learning and deep immersion in a content or topic over time.
- Sets a standard for scholarship.
- Increasingly develops skills to self-monitor and self-reflect to scrutinize for accuracy and continuous improvement.
- Promotes continuous learning.

Adapted from: Kingore, B. (2013). *Rigor and Engagement for Growing Minds*. Austin, TX: PA Publishing.

Curricular Modification

Differentiated curricula are imperative to ensure instruction that is responsive to the characteristics and needs of high-ability students. Implement specific curricular modifications that have research- and experience-based value for these students, such as:

- ☑ Inquiry and in-depth study
- ☑ Acceleration of pace and level
- ☑ Curriculum compacting
- ☑ Grouping intellectual peers
- ☑ Cluster grouped classrooms
- ☑ Tiered lessons
- ☑ Problem-based learning

Additionally, applications involving technology, mentors, and flipped classrooms promote curriculum differentiation for gifted learners of all ages as they directly influence the scope of a curriculum. Technology enables curriculum to transcend grade levels by providing seemingly limitless levels of information that surpass core curriculum to respond to individual readiness, talents, and passions. Mentors accelerate curriculum content by providing authentic expertise in a field of study. Flipped classrooms relate to curriculum compacting when their processes allow gifted students to view and master video lecture content at their best pace of learning without redundancy and escalate the level of the curriculum through video access to conceptual information exceeding grade level.

Combinations of these modifications should be evidenced in learning environments that endeavor to foster rigor and engagement in learning. A rigorous learning environment that promotes learning beyond core standards is particularly significant for high-potential students from under-represented populations. Jaime Castellano and Eva Diaz report that when high-ability or potentially gifted children from low income or culturally or linguistically diverse backgrounds experience open-ended, instructionally challenging learning experiences, their potential is stimulated and more likely to be recognized.[18]

Cluster grouping, acceleration, and curriculum compacting are paradigms with positive, sustained effects on continuous learning for advanced and gifted children. Each model is supported by abundant research and realistic implementation, yet each is dependent upon classroom teachers who differentiate skillfully.

Cluster Grouping

With cluster grouping, several high-ability students are clustered full-time in one mixed-ability classroom so a teacher can more consistently adjust instructional pace and level to their readiness. It allows gifted students to interact and learn together part of the day while encouraging a variety of grouping arrangements with all class members for the rest of the day. It is a full-time, financially sound response to the learning needs of advanced students. To clearly understand cluster grouping, read Winebrenner and Brulles's definitive book, *Cluster Grouping Handbook: How to Challenge Gifted Students and Improve Achievement for All.*[19]

Acceleration

Search the Internet using the words nation deceived and download the research from Colangelo, Assouline, and Gross entitled, *Nation Deceived: How Schools Hold Back America's Brightest Students.*[20] This outstanding report discusses the multiple kinds and significant aspects of acceleration related to high-ability students.

Curriculum Compacting

Curriculum compacting is a differentiation strategy that is highly applicable to gifted students. It is designed to eliminate redundant instruction of mastered curriculum and streamline the instructional pacing of content commensurate with students' readiness. It affords students who demonstrate high levels of achievement the time to pursue personally relevant continuous learning. An introduction to Reis and Renzulli's respected work with compacting is explained in their book *Curriculum Compacting: An Easy Start to Differentiating for High Potential Students.*[21]

Application: Replacement Tasks Motivate highly capable students to complete learning tasks in a timely fashion by implementing the routine in which students begin replacement tasks as soon as they finish quality work. With gifted learners, replacement tasks must be self-selected, interest-driven tasks that enhance conceptual understanding and construction of deeper meaning rather than enrichment tasks that merely treadmill learning by focusing on different applications of understood concepts and skills. Effective replacement tasks should allow gifted students the opportunity to pursue an ongoing, long-term commitment to an area of passion.

CHAPTER 4: ASSESSMENT TO DOCUMENT GROWTH AND INFORM INSTRUCTION

To raise the level of rigor and engagement, recognize that assessment is more than administrating tests and recording grades. The purpose of assessment is to gather dependable, accurate evidence that informs instruction and benefits students throughout an instructional segment by enabling them to demonstrate improvement and engage in continuous learning. We assess to inform instruction and promote learning, not solely to judge it.

To substantiate that students know more now than when the segment of instruction began, assessment must document that classroom learning experiences enable students to *learn and apply* something rather than only *do* something. Instead of assessments that focus on disconnected fact acquisition or repetitive skill practice, the CCSS and NGSS recommend assessments that help students construct meaningful connections for themselves and refine their ability to explain and justify their thinking to others to promote long-term memory and deeper understanding.[22] Worthy learning experiences for gifted students must represent an opportunity for a personally significant intellectual accomplishment with utilitarian value documented through quality assignments.

In reality, do we acquire valid assessment data if students perceive the evaluation process as a task to rush through so they can be done with it? To motivate advanced students to demonstrate their highest level of proficiency during assessment tasks:

- Students must understand the personal value of their assessment data, and
- Assessment procedures must be relevant and interesting enough to elicit mental and process engagement.

Documenting the Academic Growth of Gifted Learners

A key assessment question relevant to gifted learners is, "Have high-ability students demonstrated continuous learning or do high assessment results merely reflect their prior knowledge and skills?"

1. Make growth models a priority in assessment to more appropriately respond to gifted students' level and pace of learning. Solely comparing their results with grade-level standards is counterproductive to promoting advanced learning.

2. Assessments that appropriately gauge the growth of the advance learner often generate multiple pathways to success through challenging, conceptually advanced, complex, and meaningful tasks that apply previously learned concepts and skills to non-routine problems.

3. Preassessment is particularly crucial for high-ability students who frequently enter a segment of learning knowing some or all of the targeted concepts and skills. Armed with preassessment data, teachers can move gifted students to higher-level content and more complex resources that enable continuous learning and avoid the less meaningful repetition of known concepts and skills.

4. Use preassessment results to substantiate mastery and allow students the time they crave to pursue personally

relevant replacement tasks and in-depth inquiry instead of redundant work.

5. It is important to ensure that high-ability students maintain personal records of their academic progress and development as scholars. Periodically, review these self-reflections, debrief with students, and provide feedback to facilitate and support their learning as well as motivate more sophisticated work.

6. Develop the principle that excellence is much more than a grade or a grade-level comparison to standards. *Excellence* is relative to the ways in which students change as learners from their entry point of instruction to their current achievement level.

7. Empower high-ability students to develop reflective and self-assessment habits that stimulate their development as autonomous intellectual citizens. We dare not risk reinforcing gifted learners to only rely on others to inform them of the quality or deficiencies in their work.

Rubric for High Expectations of Quality

Collaborate with high-ability students to generate a set of criteria that promotes expectations for higher quality so they can document their approximations to excellence in classroom assignments and when pursuing replacement tasks. Content depth, complexity, conceptual thinking, and precise academic vocabulary are examples of criteria communicating that advanced content and deeper understanding are more important than appearance or flash value. These criteria of high quality become the main ideas for evaluations. Collaborate with students to develop rubrics, similar to the one in Figure 4.1, that incorporate these criteria and clearly communicate high expectations for advanced proficiency. After using the rubric, students write a reflection of their approximations to excellence and plan their actions for continued improvement.

RUBRIC FOR HIGH EXPECTATIONS OF QUALITY

	Grade-Level Expectations	Above Grade-Level Expectations	Advanced Response Exceeds Expectations
Content Depth	Covers topic effectively; valid content; accurate facts and details but limited depth or elaboration; conveys a general idea or understanding	Extensive and detailed study; well-developed; explores the topic beyond facts and details; elaborates key points; cites support for data	Precise, in-depth data; well-supported with multiple resources; concepts and relationships exceed grade-level; explores multifaceted information; insightful; thorough
Complexity	Simple, basic information; limited applications and critical thinking	Critical thinking is evident; compares and contrasts concepts; applies a more complicated process; supports key points	Analyzes, evaluates, adapts, and synthesizes ideas and issues across time and disciplines; logically problem solves through multiple perspectives; resources exceed grade level
Conceptual Thinking	Concrete ideas; appropriate but literal; fact and event-based thinking	Concludes connections; develops relationships with some analogous thinking; Infers; discusses concepts and principles; constructs deeper understanding	Symbolic or metaphorical; abstract thinking is evident; reasons beyond concrete realities or specific objects; poses principles or gener-alizations; idea based
Academic Vocabulary	Appropriate terminology; effective syntax and semantics	Integrates specific terminology; advanced language is clear and precise in choice and application	Vocabulary enhances the communication of complex information; integrates sophisticated words and syntax; precise terminology at a professional level

Adapted from: Kingore, B. (2013). *Rigor and Engagement for Growing Minds.* Austin, TX: PA Publishing.

Relevant, Authentic Assessments

More authentic ways to assess learning must follow implementation of authentic learning tasks. When gifted students assume the roles of authors, historians, mathematicians, or artists, for example, the question becomes, "What kinds of products should be expected from practitioners in a field of study?" Rich learning tasks, such as performances and presentations that assess how students think and respond like experts in a profession may supersede testing as more valid assessments. All ages of students with high potential can demonstrate advanced levels of achievements through authors' chairs, gallery walks, digital presentations, videos, original content-related games, physical models, presentations, musical compositions, or demonstrations of original experiments and math proofs.

Integrate Assessment Procedures
Preassessment techniques provide the baseline data that enlighten potential insights from formative and summative assessments, empowering students and teachers to analyze growth and changes as learners. The CCSS and NGSS recommend more extensive use of preassessment and formative assessment to provide feedback over time of students' growth during a learning segment and increase success on summative assessments.[23]

Some assessment procedures are applicable as both formative and summative tools. For example, incorporating peer editing or including a revise-and-resubmit step when students work on research, graphics, or written tasks provides them with feedback for recommended revisions (formative assessment) prior to submitting the final product (summative assessment).

Consolidate preassessment and formative assessment in a sequenced assessment process. After students complete a preassessment in one color ink, they return to that same document later in the learning cycle, using a second color ink to review, change, correct, add, and elaborate content on their preassessment. Encourage students to compare and contrast their learning results so far and then set goals for their next step in this learning segment. Students either revisit this assessment again later in the learning cycle or file their results as documentation of mastery and readiness to begin replacement tasks and continue learning. Teachers can use another color to mark their evaluation on the same copy and promote an atmosphere of collaboration and shared responsibility.

- Use the results from the sequenced assessment process of preassessment and formative assessment to communicate assessment information and student growth with parents or family members. This integrated process enables families to understand the academic progress of their children.
- Communicate high expectations through significant criteria that guide students as they complete assessments. Providing brief checklists, such as the one displayed in Figure 4.2, can stimulate students' effort and greater attention to content on assessment tasks. Ask students to set goals as they begin assessments by checking each level they intended to achieve.

Formative Assessment

Carol Dweck's research concludes that effective feedback is crucial to student effort and learning.[24] Use formative assessment to check for advanced insights or misconceptions early and often in a segment of learning, and offer effort-based encouragement rather than discouragement. "Your effort is obvious. Together, let's figure out what to do differently or another way to approach this."

Figure 4.2:
Assessment Checklist

Comprehension
- ☐ Blank or unintelligible
- ☐ Understandable
- ☐ Planned and organized for clarity and understanding

Content
- ☐ No or little applicable content
- ☐ Content is basic but accurate
- ☐ Content is more specific and complex

Effort
- ☐ No effort is evident
- ☐ Minimal effort; completes task
- ☐ Effort and high-level thinking are evident

Teachers' efficiency with formative assessment is directly related to students' proficiency with summative assessment. There will be few surprises in test results when teachers routinely and effectively assess understanding during instruction, and then review the results after class to guide instruction and aid grouping decisions for the next lesson. Collaborate with colleagues to develop examples of formative assessments most applicable to you, your students, and your teaching situation. Include some assessments similar to the following examples that are quick and fruitful–simple to prepare and apply but result in actionable data to facilitate immediate adjustments to instruction.

Error Investigation

At the closure of a specific skill lesson, provide content with related skill errors purposely planted in it. Challenge pairs of students to think about the skill and write responses on sticky notes as they identify, explain, and correct the errors. This assessment technique is engaging, as many students respond enthusiastically to finding others' errors. After two minutes, ask students to share and compare what they found and then post the sticky notes on the wall or door as they exit for your review after class.

I Notice... I Feel... I Want... I Think... Because...

These open-ended thinking prompts elicit students' written reflections and perceptions. Adding *because* to each prompt requires students to provide evidence and explain. Assigning two or more of the sentence stems usually provides more information; however, assign only one prompt when time is of the essence. Students can complete this reflection when concluding a discussion, ending a direct-teaching lesson, finishing a small-group task, completing silent reading, or reviewing homework.

Every-Student-Response Tools

Individual wipe-off boards, laminated card stock, or technological devices invite each student to respond to a formative assessment prompt or question, immediately supplying assessment information that informs teachers of the in-the-moment comprehension of individual students. Observe and note which students quickly record their responses, whose responses exceed expectations, who looks around for help before responding, and who would benefit from re-teaching or additional practice to increase their understanding

CONCLUSION

Continuous learning and advanced levels of achievement for advanced and gifted learners require their engagement in high-level learning processes and their demonstration of deeper understanding of relevant, sophisticated content. They need support from families, educators, and peers to pursue concepts and skills on and beyond grade-level, at a pace commensurate with their capabilities. The CCSS, NGSS, and other standards must be differentiated to ensure that gifted students flourish rather than stagnate.

Differentiate instruction to promote disciplined inquiry as students collaborate in flexible mixed-readiness groups, problem solve with groups of intellectual peers, and individually pursue topics important to their personal growth. Research substantiates that without a rigorous learning environment, gifted students risk underdevelopment of academic habits of mind due to less need for the struggle or persistence that promotes advanced learning.

1. Differentiate standards to continuously develop high-level cognitive skills while promoting relevant high-level expectations, complexity, and depth in content, process, and product.

2. Refine assessments to ensure actionable data that guides instruction and benefits all learners while enabling gifted students to appropriately accelerate their learning pace and level.

3. Promote frequent assessment to ensure that gifted students experience continuous learning and maintain records of progress reflecting personal changes as learners rather than gauge their results through comparisons with grade-level peers.

4. Implement practical, research- and evidence-based strategies that proactively differentiate for gifted learners to increase their engagement, promote personally significant intellectual accomplishments, motivate excellence, and execute standards with intellectual integrity.

ENDNOTES

[1]Gewertz, C. (2013). Standards worrying teachers. *Education Week*, 32, 1.

[2]Sprenger, M. (2013). *Teaching the critical vocabulary of the Common Core: 55 words that make or break student understanding.* Alexandria VA: Association for Supervision & Curriculum Development.

[3]Crockett, L., Jukes, I., & Churches, A. (2011). *Literacy is not enough: 21st century fluencies for the digital age.* Thousand Oaks, CA: Corwin Press; Prensky, M. (2013). Our brains extended. *Educational Leadership, 70*, 22-27.

[4]Gifford, M., & Gore, S. (2008*). The effects of focused academic vocabulary instruction on underperforming math students.* Alexandria, VA: Association for Supervision & Curriculum Development.

[5]Stronge, J.H. (2007). *Qualities of effective teachers (2nd ed.).* Alexandria VA: Association for Supervision & Curriculum Development.

[6]Noddings, N. (2009). All our students thinking. In M. Scherer (Ed.), *Engaging the whole child: Reflections on best practices in learning, teaching and leadership.* Alexandria, VA: Association for Supervision & Curriculum Development.

[7]Dean, C., Hubbell, E., Pitler, H., & Stone, B. (2012). *Classroom instruction that works: Research-based strategies for increasing student achievement* (2nd ed.). Alexandria, VA: Association for Supervision & Curriculum Development.

[8]Willis, J. (2010). The current impact of neuroscience on teaching and learning. In D. Sousa, *Mind, brain, & education: Neuroscience implications for the classroom* (pp. 45-68). Bloomington, IN: Solution Tree Press.

[9]Dean, C., Hubbell, E., Pitler, H., & Stone, B. (2012).

[10]Medina, J. (2009). *Brain rules: 12 principles for surviving and thriving at work, home, and school.* Seattle, WA: Pear Press; Sousa, D., & Tomlinson, C. (2010). *Differentiation and the brain: How neuroscience supports the learner-friendly*

classroom. Bloomington, IN: Solution Tree Press; Willis, J. (2010).

[11]McTighe, J., & O'Connor, K. (2005). Seven practices for effective learning. *Educational Leadership*, 63, 10-17.

[12]Sousa, D. (2009). *How the gifted brain learns* (2nd ed.). Thousand Oaks, CA: Corwin Press.

[13]Medina, J. (2009); Sousa, D. (2009); Sousa, D. & Tomlinson, C. (2010); Willis, J. (2007*). Brain-friendly strategies for the inclusion classroom.* Alexandria, VA: Association for Supervision & Curriculum Development; Willis, J. (2010)

[14]Jones, R. (2008). *Strengthening student engagement.* Rexford, NY: International Center for Leadership in Education.

[15]Elias, M. (2012). *SEL and whole child education: An essential partnership.* Social-Emotional Learning Lab. Retrieved from http://www.edutopia.org

[16]Stiggins, R. & Chappuis, J. (2011). *An introduction to student-involved assessment for learning* (6th ed.). Boston, MA: Pearson Education.

[17]Center for Authentic Intellectual Work. (2012). *Criteria and standards for authentic pedagogy and student work.* Retrieved from http://centerforaiw.com

[18]Castellano, J. A. & Diaz, E. I. (Eds.). (2002). *Reaching new horizons: Gifted and talented education for culturally and linguistically diverse students.* Boston: Allyn & Bacon.

[19]Winebrenner, S., & Brulles, D. (2008*). Cluster grouping handbook: How to challenge gifted students and improve achievement for all.* Minneapolis, MN: Free Spirit Publishing.

[20]Colangelo, N., Assouline, S., & Gross, M. (2004*). A nation deceived: How schools hold back America's brightest students.* Iowa City: University of Iowa, Belin & Blank International Center for Gifted Education and Talent Development.

[21]Reis, S. & Renzulli, J. (2005). *Curriculum compacting: An easy start to differentiating for high potential students.* Waco, TX: Prufrock Press.

[22]National Academy of Sciences. (2013). *Next Generation Science Standards: For states, by states.* Washington, DC: National Academies Press; National Governors Association Center for Best Practices, & Council of Chief State School Officers. (2010a). *Common core state standards for English language arts and literacy in history/social studies, science, and technical subjects.* Retrieved from

http://www.corestandards.org; National Governors
Association Center for Best Practices, & Council of Chief State
School Officers. (2010b). *Common core state standards for Mathematics.* Retrieved from http://www.corestandards.org.

[23]National Academy of Sciences (2013); National Governors
Association Center for Best Practices, & Council of Chief State
School Officers (2010a), (2010b).

[24]Dweck, C. (2006). *Mindset: The new psychology of success.* New
York, NY: Random House; Dweck, C. (2010). Giving students
meaningful work: Even geniuses work hard. *Educational Leadership,* 68, 16-20.

KEY RESOURCES

Adams, C. M., Cotabish, A., & Ricci, M. C. (2014). *Using the Next Generation Science Standards with gifted and advanced* learners. Waco, TX: Prufrock Press.

This work differentiates science learning experiences highly able K-12 learners. The book describes strategies and effective differentiated activities for implementing rigor and relevance.

Colangelo, N., Assouline, S., & Gross, M. (2004). *A nation deceived: How schools hold back America's brightest students.* Iowa City: University of Iowa, Belin & Blank International Center for Gifted Education and Talent Development.

This report chronicles crucial implications regarding differentiation for gifted students. It is the definitive discussion of the multiple kinds and significant aspects of acceleration related to rigor for high-ability students.

Hughes, C. E., Kettler, T., Shaunessy-Dedrick, E., & VanTassel-Baska, J. (2014). *A teacher's guide to using the Common Core State Standards with gifted and advanced learners in English language arts.* Waco, TX: Prufrock Press.

This work differentiates English language arts learning experiences for K-12 highly able learners. It describes strategies and effective differentiated activities for implementing rigor and relevance within today's standards.

Note: See also VanTassel-Baska, J. (Ed.). (2013). *Using the Common Core State Standards for English language arts with* *gifted and advanced learners*. Waco, TX: Prufrock Press.

Johnsen, S. K., Ryser, G. R., & Assouline, S. G. (2014). *A teachers guide to using the Common Core State Standards with mathematically gifted and advanced students*. Waco, TX: Prufrock Press.

This work differentiates learning experiences in mathematics for highly able learners. Strategies and effective differentiated activities are described for implementing rigor in mathematics in K-12 schools.

Note: See also Johnsen, S., & Sheffield, L. (Eds.). (2013). *Using the Common Core State Standards for mathematics with gifted and advanced learners.* Waco, TX: Prufrock Press.

Kingore, B. (2013.) *Rigor and engagement for growing minds: Strategies that enable high-ability learners to flourish in all classrooms*. Austin, TX: PA Publishing.

This award-winning book enables educators to realistically transform classrooms into rigorous learning environments. Practical strategies and hundreds of examples guide teachers to uplift standards for high-ability students while transforming lessons and products with rigor, relevance, and higher levels of thinking.

Tomlinson, C., & Imbeau, M. (2010). *Leading and managing a differentiated classroom*. Alexandria VA: Association for Supervision & Curriculum Development.

Management concerns limit some teachers' differentiation efforts. This book tackles this issue by addressing student differences and focuses on specific ways teachers and students collaborate for a differentiated classroom that is student-focused and responsive.

ABOUT THE AUTHORS

Bertie Kingore, Ph.D. is an international consultant, a visiting professor and speaker at numerous universities, as well as an award-winning author of 27 books. A former classroom teacher, she has worked in classrooms from preschool through graduate school. She and her husband Richard are the parents of three gifted sons.

ABOUT THE SERIES EDITOR

Cheryll M. Adams, Ph.D., is the Director Emerita of the Center for Gifted Studies and Talent Development at Ball State University. She has served on the Board of Directors of NAGC and has been president of the Indiana Association for the Gifted and the Association for the Gifted, Council for Exceptional Children.

Made in the USA
Lexington, KY
10 July 2017